Love Transcends
Text copyright © Kimby Shult Hughes 2017

Images copyright © Mike and Heather Krakora of Krakora Studios, Inc. 2017
www.krakorastudios.com

All Rights Reserved. No part of this book may be reproduced, transmitted or stored in an information retrieval system in any means, graphic, electronic or mechanical, including photocopying, taping or recording, without prior written permission from the publisher.

Published in the United States by E&P Publishing, LLC
P.O. Box 45632
Madison, WI 53744

Printed in the United States of America

ISBN 978-0-9987235-0-1 (p)
ISBN 978-0-9987235-1-8 (h)
ISBN 978-0-9987235-2-5 (e)

Library of Congress Control Number: 2017933887

is dedicated to:
My children, Elijah and Penelope. I am blessed by your authenticity and joy. You are daily reminders of God's love and goodness!

Kimby Shult Hughes

Photography By
Heather & Michael Krakora

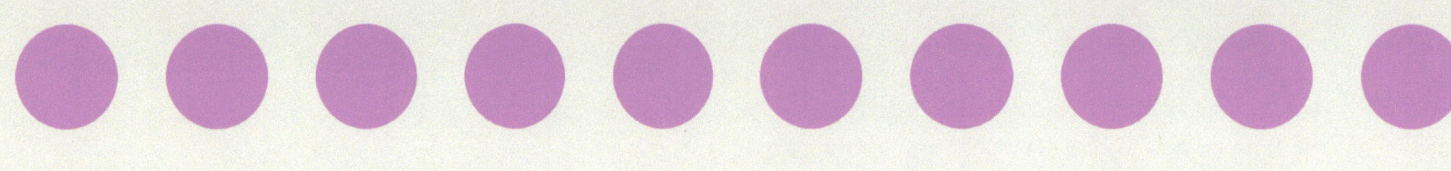

Special thanks to:
My husband, Nick, for being my best friend, a wonderful father,
and for all of his hard work on this book.

Our adoption social worker for her knowledge and compassion
while guiding us through the adoption process.

The mindful teachers who facilitate space for children and families
to authentically engage difficult topics.

The people God uses to shape, heal, and grow
my family and me!

A note from the author:
This book was inspired by a conversation I had with my son, Elijah.
Conversations about adoption, race, gender, privilege, and faith
have been a part of our family since our children were infants.
One afternoon, Elijah initiated a conversation about these things.
He was two years old at the time. That conversation became this book.
Though I penned it, this is Elijah's story. One I am honored
to help him tell. These are his thoughts. These are his emotions. This is his life.
However you find your way to this book, may you be blessed by it.

My name is Elijah.

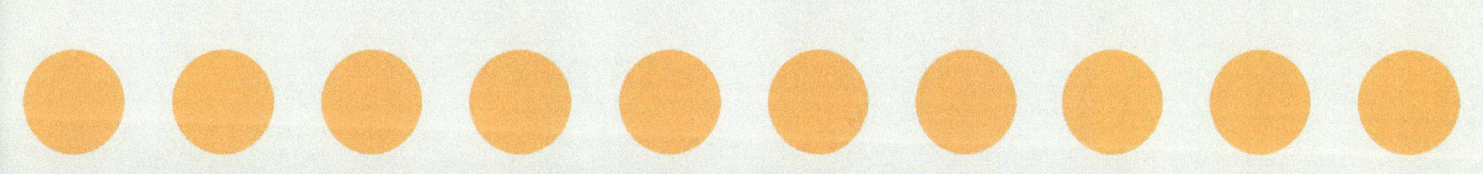

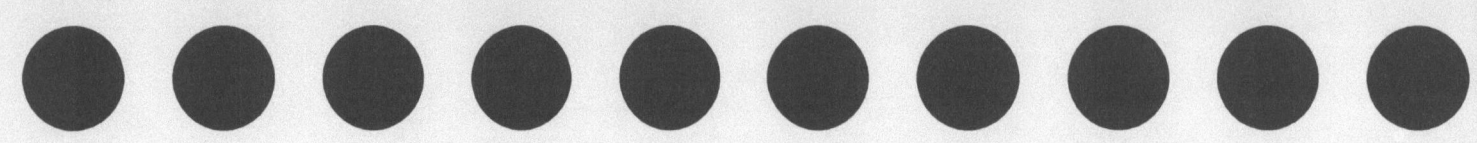

I'm two.
Well, almost three.
Most days of my life
I'm as happy as can be.

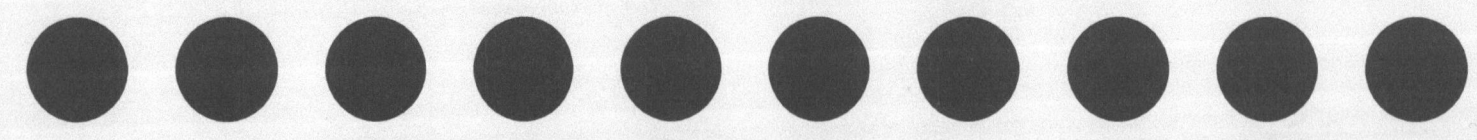

When I'm running, I go fast.
And rarely stop to rest.

I love to play and dance. Singing is the best.

Even though
I laugh and smile
through the day and night...

At times I feel other things,
and Mama tells me,
"That's all right."

Sometimes I feel scared.
Dada says,
"My son,
that's okay."

Sometimes I feel angry.
I want to
let it out
in productive ways.

But lately I've been feeling something
that's a bit new to me.
I've been feeling really different
in ways everyone can see.

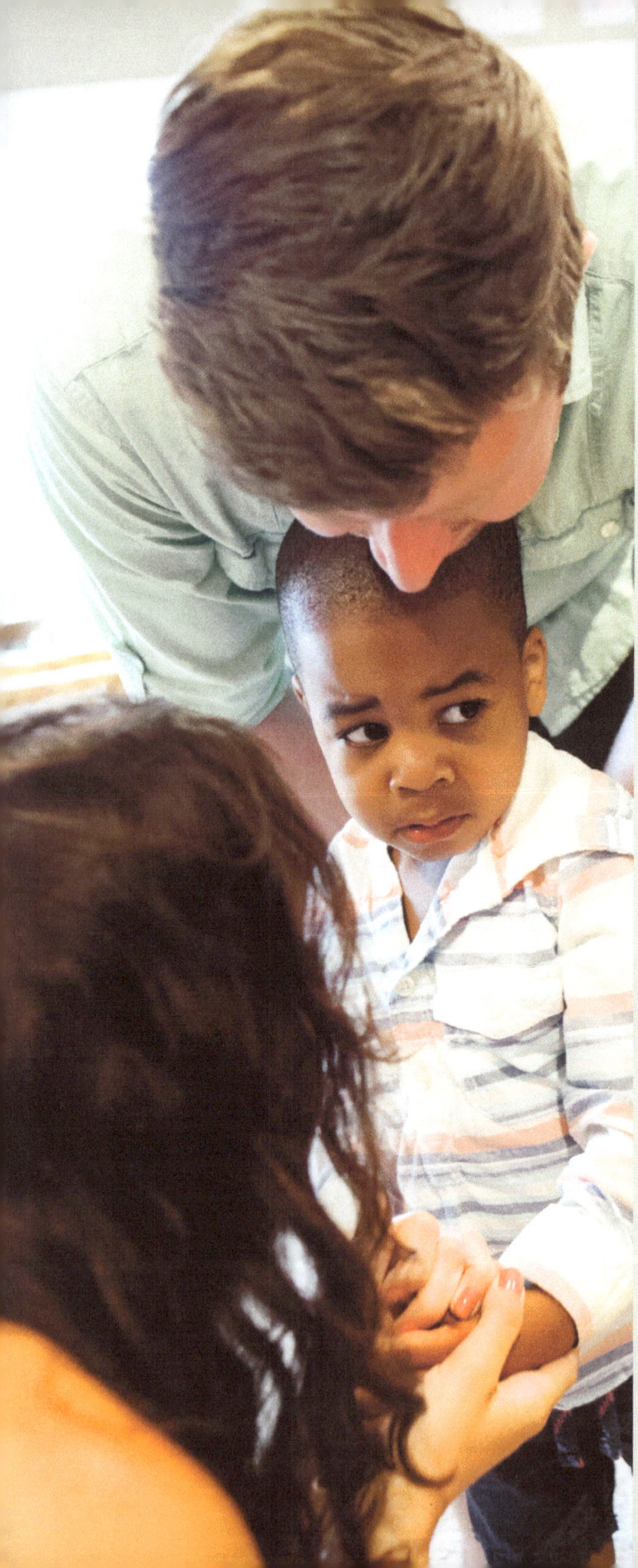

I told Mama today,
"I don't look the same as you."
And I said it in a tone
that was less than enthused.

Mama asked how that made me feel,
I told her, "I'm pretty sad."
You see, it's hard to look so different from
the only family I've ever had.

My family is all white.
I have brown skin.

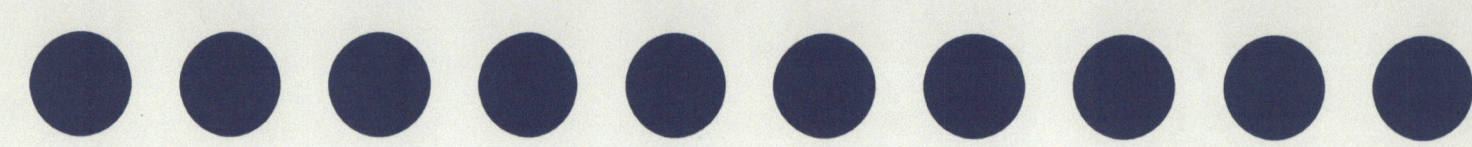

My lips are full.
My sister's are pretty thin.

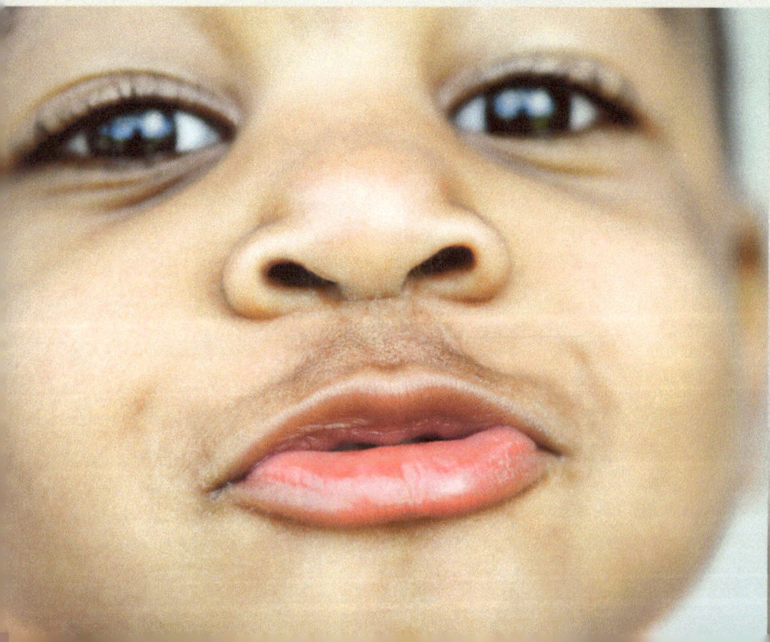

I feel Sister's hair.
Then Mama's and Dada's too.
And I tell them once again,
"See, I'm not the same as you."

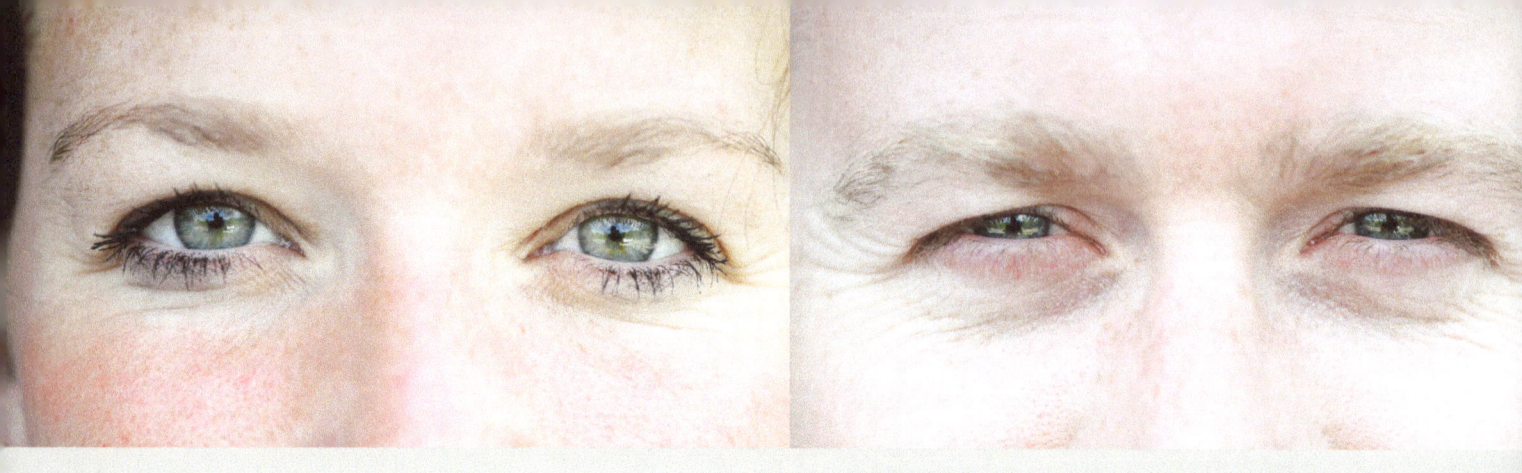

I look into my parents' eyes.
I see only green and blue.
I look into the mirror and say,
"See, nobody has brown like you."

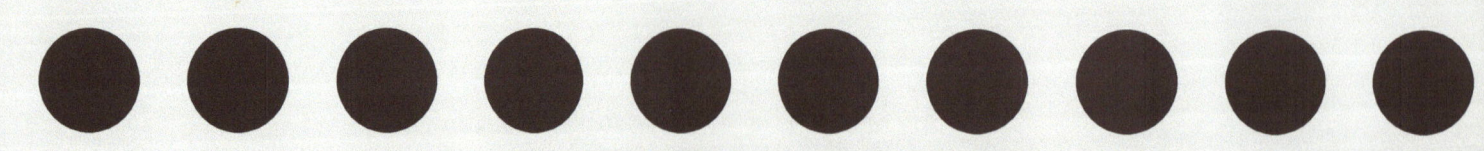

My parents remind me I am beautiful.
Every part of me.
That God chose me to be their son.
And they are my family.

Mama reminds me that I feel deeply.
She also feels in that way.
We are both strong leaders,
guiding others every day.

Dada is always observing.
He loves to explore, just like me.
So, I guess in that way,
we are as similar as can be.

I admit that I'm a bit loud
in my voice and personality.
Sister is the same
and admits to that reality.

Just like me,
Mama loves to dance.
She twirls and
tosses me high.

In that moment,
I remember our likeness,
as we dance
side by side.

Dada loves the outdoors.
I enjoy nature every day.
We could stay out there forever.
That makes us the same.

Mama and I are athletic.
God just made us that way.

I'm reminded how similar we are, when we run, jump, and play.

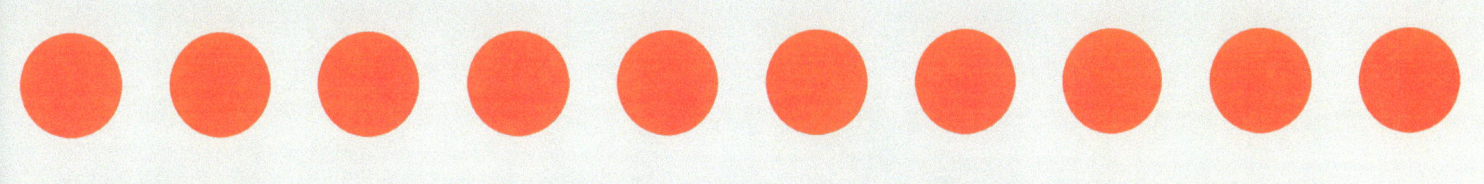

Sister loves to play pretend.
I am imaginative too.
We ride off together to save the day,
doing what superheroes do.

Dada and I love to be silly,
with our humor and tickles too.
As we laugh together he says,
"My son, I'm a lot like you."

I express myself
through music.
I have from
the very start.

Mama writes me songs about how I've always been in her heart.

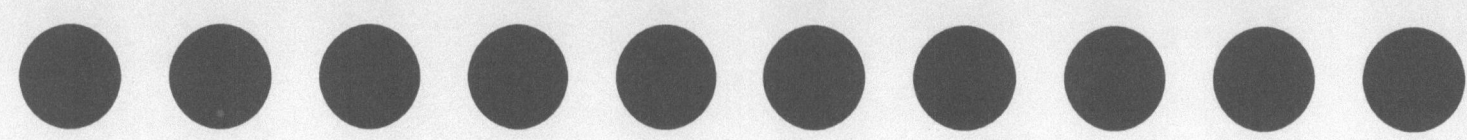

After talking about these things
Mama asks, "Are you still feeling sad?"
And I realize in that moment,
I no longer feel as bad.

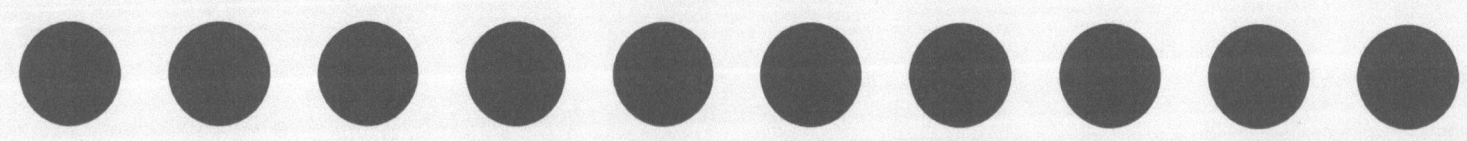

Because even though I look different
in the obvious ways you can see,
I'm so much like my family,
when you get to know all of me.

I want to remind you that
I often wrestle with these things.
Feeling different is a challenge.
It's what my beautiful life brings.

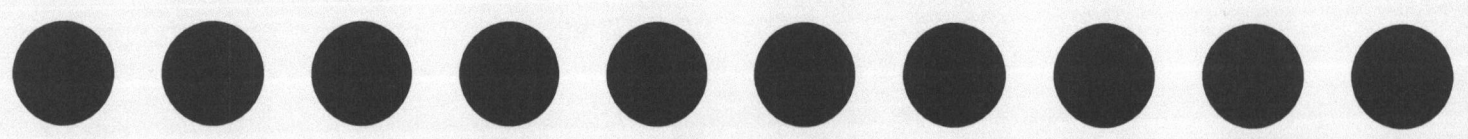

Please just let me say it.
Please let me feel
what I need to feel.
My anger and my sadness
are important.
They are real.

At times I'll need reminders
to celebrate the uniqueness of me.
To embrace the ways I'm different,
both the obvious and the unseen.

At times I'll need reminders
that I belong in this family.
Your love for me is unending.
I'm free to just be me.

I found my way to my family,
not by chance or accident.
The love that transcends our differences
is undoubtedly heaven-sent.

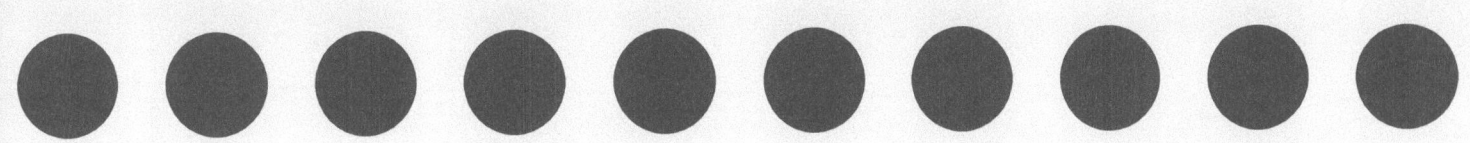

There's a joy that shines so brightly.
It connects my family.
I hope that you have felt it,
as I've told you all about me.